ST. FRANCIS OF ASSISI
A HUMBLE SERVANT OF GOD

Divon Le

A JOURNEY OF FAITH, HUMILITY, AND PEACE

St. Francis of Assisi: A Humble Servant of God
A Journey of Faith, Humility, and Peace

ISBN (Paperback): 979-8-9943825-3-0
ISBN (Hardcover): 979-8-9943825-4-7

Series: Radiant Saint Stories, Book 2

Published by
Radiant Faith Press

First Edition

On the 800th anniversary of Saint Francis's holy death, this work is offered in humble gratitude for a life that still speaks across the centuries, calling hearts to simplicity, joy, mercy, and total surrender to God.

His life became a living mirror of the Gospel. May the witness of these pages draw all who read them closer to Christ, the one Love who never ends.

A CHILD BENEATH ASSISI'S SKIES

Beneath Assisi's humble skies,
A child is born with wondering eyes.
Francis, called to a holy quest,
To seek the Lord above the rest.
A path of change he will embrace,
In time, to lead with love and grace.

DID YOU KNOW?

Saint Francis was baptized Giovanni, but his father later called him
Francesco, meaning "Frenchman," because he loved France and its culture.

A JOYFUL YOUNG FRANCIS

In lovely clothes, with songs and cheer,
Young Francis held his pleasures dear.
He dreamed of feasts and worldly fame,
Yet God still softly called his name.

✝

O Lord, when our hearts start to stray,
Please draw us gently back Your way.

A YOUNG KNIGHT'S DREAM

When war with Perugia filled the land,
Young Francis took his armor in his hand.
He marched with courage, hoping for fame,
Not knowing God had a different aim.

*Lord, teach us that true greatness shines,
Not in pride, but in a Will like Thine.*

A YEAR BEHIND PRISON WALLS

The battle lost, his freedom torn away,
Captured and held, awaiting ransom's day.
In prison dark, with sorrow in the air,
He saw the grief that many souls must bear.
Within those walls, where nights were long and deep,
God stirred the heart He longed to keep.

✝

O Lord, in trials when we are weak,
Guide us to the peace we truly seek.

THE LONGING IN HIS HEART

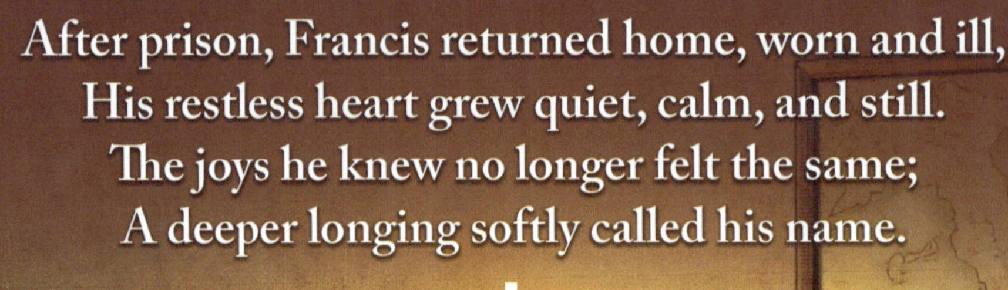

After prison, Francis returned home, worn and ill,
His restless heart grew quiet, calm, and still.
The joys he knew no longer felt the same;
A deeper longing softly called his name.

✝

Lord, when our hearts are ill at rest,
Let longing for You make us blest.

13

After recovering from illness, Francis tried once more to become a knight.
But in Spoleto, God spoke to him in a dream and changed the direction of his life.

THE DREAM AT SPOLETO

When health came back, his dreams grew bold:
Of knightly honor, praise, and gold.
Though grace had touched his soul to pray,
He turned to war and rode away.

But God spoke through a dream that night,
And turned his heart from earthly might:

"Why serve the servant, leave the Master true?"
And changed the dreams his young heart knew.
He left behind his dreams of knightly glory,
To follow Christ and live a greater story.

·············· ✝ ··············

O Christ, when earthly hopes decay,
Remind our hearts that You are the Way.

FRANCIS RETURNS HOME & THE CROSS AT SAN DAMIANO

His heart felt restless, his old joys grew dim,
Till he embraced the leper and saw Christ in him.
Before a worn wooden cross he knelt to pray,
Christ's voice broke through that sacred day:
"Go, Francis, and rebuild My Church," He said,
And those words sank deep, like seeds well spread.

························ ✝ ·························

Lord, help us hear when You have spoken,
And mend what in Your Church lies broken.

GIVING UP ALL FOR GOD

He sold his father's goods to mend God's place,
And brought deep grief to his father's face.
Before the bishop, his father made his plea,
Francis gave back all, and stood there free.
With nothing left, no home, no claim,
He called God Father and praised His name.

O Lord, unbind our hearts from earthly strings,
And clothe us in the joy Your love now brings.

POOR IN THE WORLD, RICH IN GOD

In the square, with nothing left to own,
Young Francis stood by grace alone.
The bishop wrapped him, kind and mild,
And blessed him as God's holy child.

Lord, when the world leaves us poor,
Teach us that You are wealth forevermore.

FRANCIS BEGINS TO REBUILD

Restoring chapels old and worn,
With faithful hands from early morn.
He lived on prayer and humble bread,
And followed where the Savior led.

.... ✝ ....

O God, make us like Francis, gentle and free,
To serve with childlike trust in Thee.

BROTHERS BEGIN TO GATHER

His humble life drew others near,
Not through riches, power, or fear.
They chose the path of poverty,
To live in peace and charity.

Lord, gather us in love, and lead
Our hearts to serve each other's need.

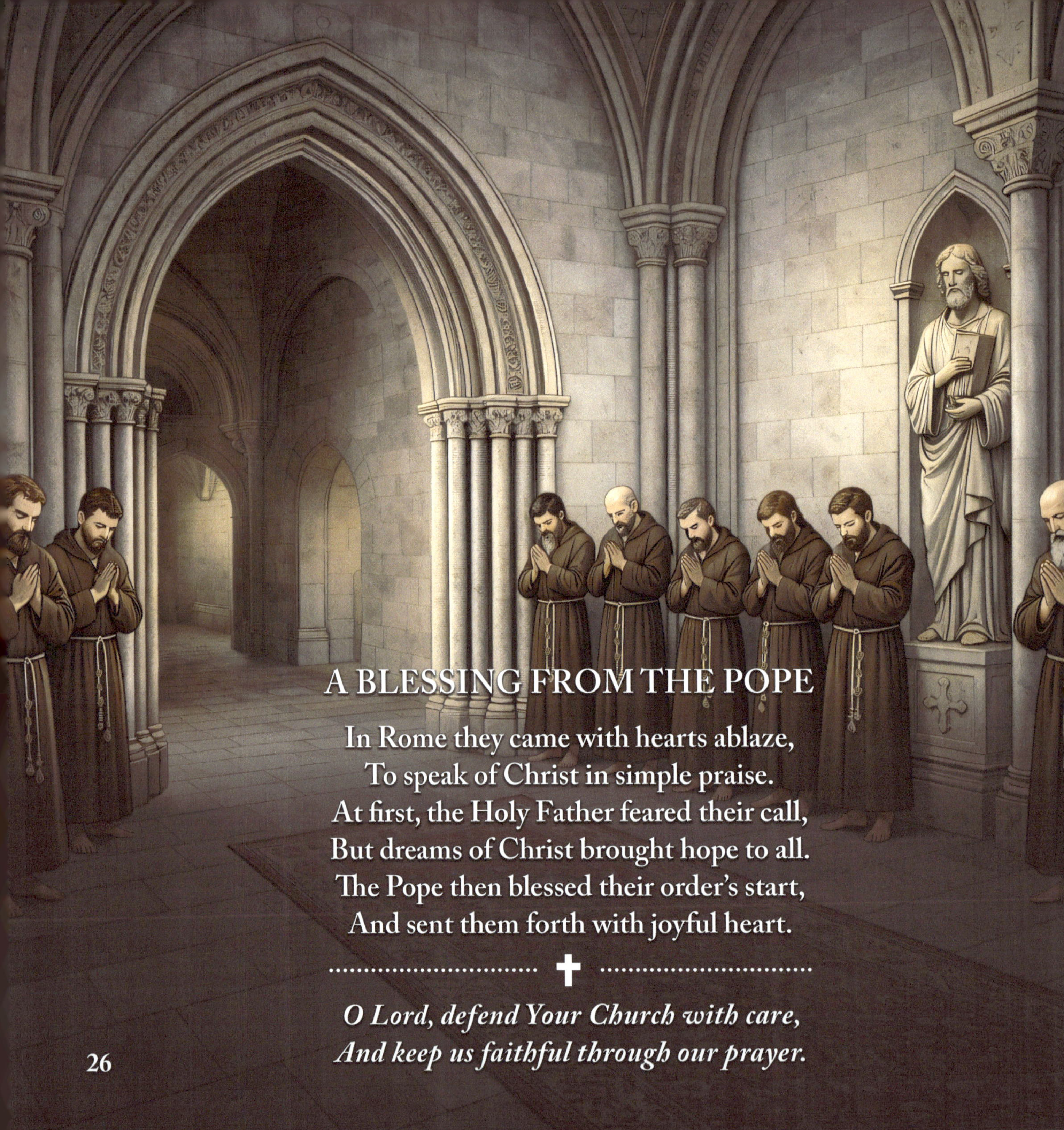

A BLESSING FROM THE POPE

In Rome they came with hearts ablaze,
To speak of Christ in simple praise.
At first, the Holy Father feared their call,
But dreams of Christ brought hope to all.
The Pope then blessed their order's start,
And sent them forth with joyful heart.

✝

O Lord, defend Your Church with care,
And keep us faithful through our prayer.

PREACHING THE GOSPEL WITH JOY

Through towns and fields, the friars went,
To preach God's mercy where they were sent.
With barefoot steps the brothers trod,
They called lost hearts to turn to God.

✝

Lord, may our words and actions both proclaim
The saving sweetness of Your Holy Name.

CLARE JOINS FRANCIS TO FOLLOW CHRIST

A noble maiden heard God's call,
And longed to give Him heart and all.
One Palm Sunday, beneath the night,
Clare left her home to follow Light.
With Francis there, that holy day,
She made her vow to Christ's poor way.

†

O Lord, give us a heart made new,
To seek Your love in all we do.

DID YOU KNOW?

Clare was a noble young woman from Assisi who admired Francis's humility and his love for God. On the night of Palm Sunday, she quietly left home to give her life fully to Christ. That same evening, she made her vow and had her hair cut by candlelight. She became the first woman to follow Francis and later led the Poor Clares, an order of sisters who lived in prayer and poverty.

FRANCIS AMONG THE PEOPLE

Through hills and valleys he trod,
Helping the weary turn to God.
His face shone bright for all to see,
A sign of love and charity.

*Lord, may our kindness, pure and true,
Gently lead all hearts to You.*

33

PREACHING PEACE AT THE FIFTH CRUSADE

In distant lands of war and strife,
He crossed the lines to speak of life.
He met the Sultan, face to face,
And spoke of peace with calm and grace.

✝

O Christ, where hatred clouds our mind,
Let humble hearts bring love to all mankind.

DID YOU KNOW?
During the Fifth Crusade, Francis crossed enemy lines to
meet Sultan Malik al-Kamil. Moved by Francis's courage
and conviction, the Sultan received him graciously and
allowed him to preach for a time before returning safely.

HOME TO ITALY;
BROTHER WOLF AWAITS

When Francis journeyed home once more,
A frightened town had locked each door.
A wolf brought fear to Gubbio's town,
Yet Francis met and calmed it down.
With gentle voice, he made Brother Wolf agree,
To harm no more, but live in harmony.

Lord, teach our hearts to answer hurt with peace,
So fear and anger may decrease.

FRANCIS CREATES THE FIRST CHRISTMAS MANGER

At Greccio, on a blessed Christmas night,
He set a manger scene to bring delight.
The ox and lamb beside the newborn King,
Moved hearts to pray and sweetly sing.

·················· ✝ ··················

Lord Jesus, born in poverty,
Make in our hearts Your home to be.

DID YOU KNOW?

Francis is credited with creating the first live Nativity
scene. He wanted people to see the humble place where
Jesus was born. Today, families and churches around the
world continue this beautiful Christmas tradition.

39

THE FRANCISCAN WAY OF LIFE

He shaped a rule of Gospel, work, and prayer,
For brothers called to serve and share.
Though many came, he sought no throne,
But hearts that lived for Christ alone.

O Lord, as duties fill our hand,
Let humble love in all things stand.

40

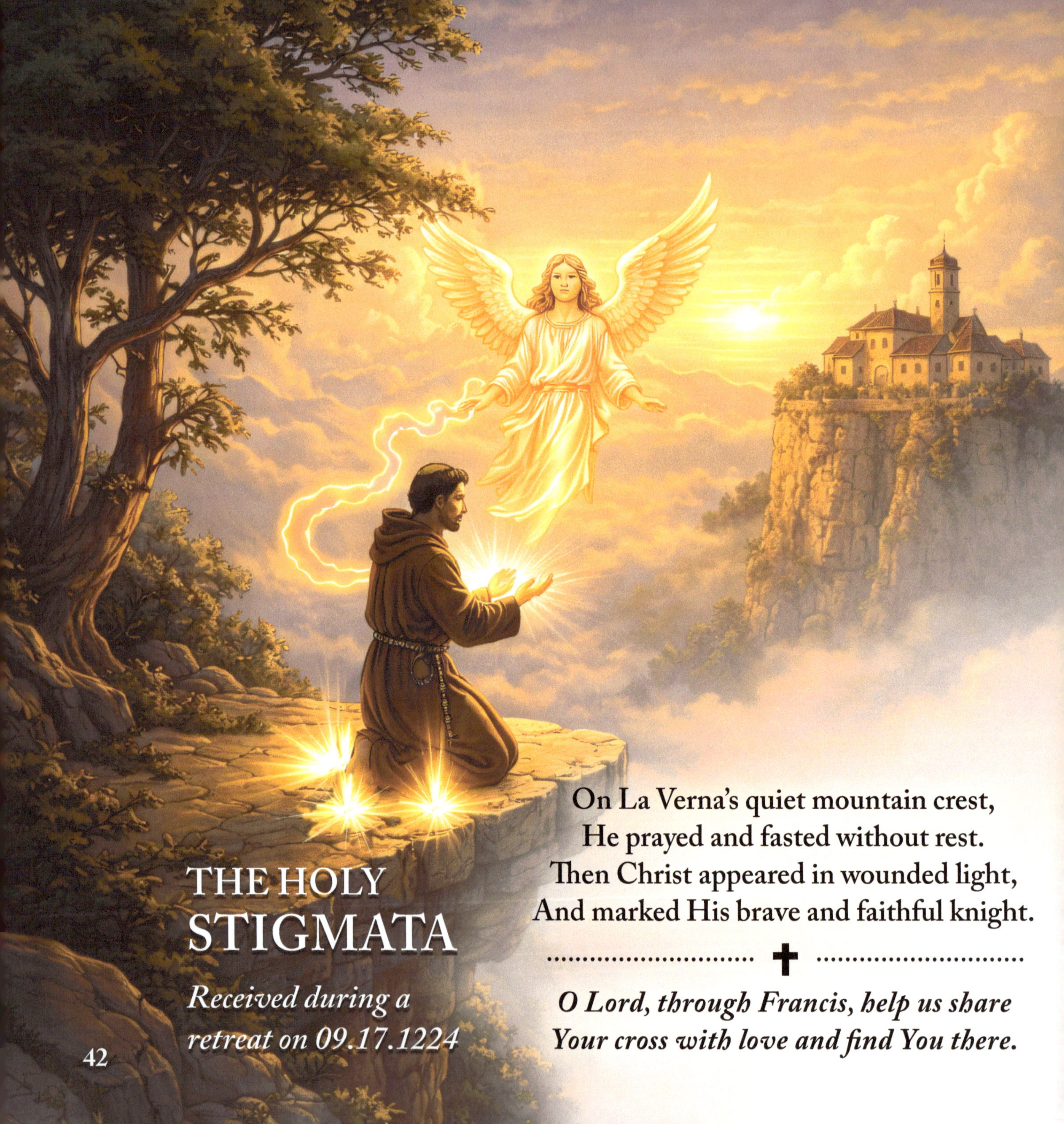

THE HOLY
STIGMATA

Received during a retreat on 09.17.1224

On La Verna's quiet mountain crest,
He prayed and fasted without rest.
Then Christ appeared in wounded light,
And marked His brave and faithful knight.

*O Lord, through Francis, help us share
Your cross with love and find You there.*

DID YOU KNOW?
Francis received the stigmata, the wounds of Christ, while praying and fasting for forty days on Mount La Verna.

FRANCIS SINGS HIS FINAL PRAISE

Though weak in body, Francis sang with grace,
His Canticle of the Sun in that quiet place.
For sun and moon and stars so bright,
He praised the Lord with all his might.
Then Sister Death drew gently near,
And Francis praised Christ without fear.

Lord, lead us when our days are through,
To sing Your praise and be with You.

FRANCIS OF ASSISI
left his earthly life

✝

10.03.1226

CANONIZED A SAINT *by Pope Gregory IX*

☦

07.16.1228

DID YOU KNOW?

The grand Basilica of St. Francis of Assisi began the day after Francis became a saint, when Pope Gregory IX laid the first stone.

45

SCAN to view
series on Amazon

RADIANT SAINT STORIES

The Radiant Saint Stories Series introduces young readers to the inspiring lives of holy men and women who followed Christ with courage, faith, and love.

Through engaging storytelling and beautiful illustrations, these books help children discover the saints as friends, role models, and companions on the path to heaven.

BOOKS IN THE SERIES

Available Now

Book 1. Philomena: The Brave Daughter of Light
A courageous young martyr whose faith shines brighter than fear.

Book 2. St. Francis of Assisi: A Humble Servant of God
A Journey of Faith, Humility, and Peace. An inspiring story of a beloved saint who embraced poverty and taught the world to love God and all creation.

Book 3. Carlo Acutis: Jeans, Sneakers, and a Saint
The First Millennial Saint, a tech-savvy teenager who made the Eucharist his life's mission and became a saint.

Coming Soon

St. Therese of Lisieux (Fall 2026), **St. Patrick, St. Padre Pio, St. Joan of Arc, and more...**

Divon Le
Author & Designer

Divon is an award-winning visual media professional with more than 25 years of experience in design, illustration, multimedia, and 3D animation. Through storytelling and visual communication, he has helped clients bring complex ideas to life with clarity and purpose. He lives in the Washington, D.C. metropolitan area with his wife and two sons, where he is active in his church and community. Inspired by faith, family, and creativity, Divon hopes to create books that reveal the wonders of God, share timeless moral values, and celebrate unconditional love.

Thank you for reading!

If you enjoyed this book, please consider
leaving a 30 second review on Amazon.

Your feedback help other families learn more about
St. Francis of Assisi and support more future adventures.